Lucy and Max

A mostly true story about the amazing friendship
between a wild goose and a 'ferocious' guard dog
in Taghkanic, New York.
Could this be the modern-day version of
"Jonathan Livingston Seagull?"

by Dan Udell

by Dan Udell

Udell Books

Published by Udell Communications

397 Old State Route 82

Taghkanic, New York 12521

Manufactured in the USA

ISBN-13: 9781530663866
ISBN-10: 1530663865

To Seanne, Brian, Moira and Kevin.
For believing in me.
Finally, a bedtime story for you and all
the children of the world.
A story to believe in.

And thanks to Mary and her three
daughters, Laurie, Heidi and Dana for
their support and encouragement.

Acknowledgments

Where to begin. Of course, my mother, Martha, a very talented person who taught me so much about how to translate my ideas into reality -- and the joy of creation. Most recently, my children: Seanne, Brian, Moira and Kevin: four wonderful people in whom I am very proud. They found the key that was necessary to unlock what was inside me and to write it down. I wrote for IBM as a science and technology writer for decades, but couldn't find the voice to express my own feelings. I remember my mother saying many times, "Danny, why wasn't your name mentioned" in response to the many press announcements I had orchestrated and written about IBM for the NY Times and other media. It was a logical question, but I could never provide an answer that would satisfy her.

Then, there is Mary, my dear wife, friend, lover, critic, confidant and proofreader. And not incidentally, the mother of three wonderful daughters: Laurie, Heidi and Dana. I learned about how to express my feelings simply by observing her. She is such an outgoing person with such feeling for other people, I am constantly amazed. A real humanitarian, which my brother the late Reverend C. Leland Udell of Burlington, VT first observed a few years ago. And significantly, Mary is a wonderful arts curator and long-time gallery director, where she provided a platform for me to express myself in photography, and not incidentally, design and print many, many fliers, posters and brochures to bring the gallery's artists to the attention of thousands of arts lovers.

And then, there is nature and the animal kingdom. They were my true friends in my childhood years. Those feelings have stayed with me, and I guess that's pretty obvious from the 'Lucy & Max' story.

In closing, we dedicate this book to all our 14 grandchildren* and Lisa Dolan, director of the successful 'Hudson Reads' program at the M.C. Smith School in Hudson, NY -- providing reading mentors for children who need help.

* Albert, Danny, Gabe, Luke, Josie, Nicky, Diane, Harrison, Annie, Claire, Dean, Morgan (Austin), Max and Ruby. And their pets. They all live along the great migration paths of Canadian Geese on the East Coast of the United States.

Dan Udell
February 26, 2016

LUCY AND MAX

A mostly true story about the amazing friendship between a wild goose and a 'ferocious' guard dog in Taghkanic, New York.

© **Dan Udell**

Lucy had a pain in her left wing, just below her shoulder. It wasn't that bad except when she was flying. This afternoon when the flock was making its way to Bell's Pond, she had trouble keeping up. When they all landed at Bell's Pond, Lucy had fallen back to last place.

That made her sad. Until only a year ago, she was the first. Always the first. And now she was last.

She worried about how she would feel tomorrow. But right now, she was content to feed off the corn droppings in Skoda's field. The kernels hadn't dried out yet and they were chewy just the way she liked them.

The great flight south to Virginia
This was fall and the flock was getting ready for its great flight south to Virginia. It was always warmer there in the winter and there was food.

And it was exciting. During the summer, Lucy and the flock spent many lazy days in the farm fields

Lucy

and frolicking and sleeping on Bell's Pond.

When they returned to Bells Pond every evening, they didn't come down with wings flapping, they glided in, with wings outstretched. A very graceful sight.
Every year at this time, things just got more serious and the daily flights got longer and higher.

The sun set over the Catskill Mountains and it got dark. All the geese crowded around each other for protection and warmth. Judy swam over to her. She was Lucy's best friend and was in the lead this afternoon.

"What happened to you today," she asked. "It's my shoulder. It hurts really bad," Lucy said. Judy replied, "I hope you'll be OK tomorrow, we're flying way down the Hudson River," and with that gave her an affectionate peck on the cheek. Judy knew because she was the leader of the flock and knew about their training flights. After a while, they both fell asleep, with their beaks tucked under their wings.

Lucy wouldn't be able to fly
When Lucy woke up the next morning, the pain in her shoulder was a lot worse. She knew she wouldn't be able to fly that day. Very soon all the

When they returned to Bells Pond every evening, they didn't come down with wings flapping, they glided in, with wings outstretched.

She began walking down the hill on a little road called Cross Street. This was very unusual for a goose because they usually don't walk on roads.

geese began making gobbling noises and climbed into the sky for their morning flight to Skoda's field for morning break-fast. It was a ritual.

Later that morning, the flock started re-turning to the pond in small groups. Lucy tried flapping her wings but it was just too painful. She was left all by herself sitting in the cornfield. This was the worst day of her life.

She just didn't know what to do. Lucy began walking. It was the only movement that didn't cause pain in her shoulder. Sko-da's cornfield was on a hill.

Geese don't walk down roads

She began walking down the hill on a little road called Cross Street. This was very unusual for a goose because they usually don't walk on roads. Actually, they don't walk that much at all. They fly and they swim and they wander around fields looking for food but they don't go very far. Because they don't walk like you or I. Instead they waddle.

Lucy had never walked on Cross Street before. She never even walked down the hill. She had never walked to "go any-where." This was a totally new experience for her.

The pond looked inviting

At the bottom of the hill she saw a tiny little pond. As she drew near, it looked

more and more inviting. It wasn't
too deep, so she would be able to fish
for nibbles on the bottom. There was
even a little stand of cattails she could
hide in. She knew that she would be
alone here and would have to take
precautions to keep herself safe.

She launched herself onto the pond.
Its waters were warm and welcoming.
Lucy began to feel better.

After fishing for food at the bottom
of the pond, Lucy hid behind the
cattails and took a nap. It felt good
to just let herself go and let her body
take over.

Lucy saw a monster of a dog
When she woke up, she looked across
the pond and saw a frightening site.
There sat a huge dog who was looking straight at her. Lucy froze.

On closer inspection, she saw that
this monster of a dog was sitting in
some kind of a house. (We would
know it as a dog house, but Lucy
had never seen one before, nor had
anyone ever told her that it was called
a dog house.)

Lucy had lived a very restricted life.
It was all centered around the flock.
And the flock kept far away from
dogs and people and all of their be-
longings like dog houses.

There sat a huge dog who was looking straight at her. Lucy froze.

"This property is guarded by Max, which is a wild, killer dog. Proceed at your own risk. I'm not responsible for death or dismemberment." Signed Jack

The dog just kept staring at Lucy, but he didn't move. And neither did Lucy. She didn't want to call attention to herself. This standoff continued for an incredible two hours. Lucy had never stayed so still in her whole life.

A wild, killer dog

Of course, Lucy couldn't read the sign over the doghouse, which the owner had nailed up, which said, "This property is guarded by Max, who is a wild, killer dog. Proceed at your own risk. I'm not responsible for death or dismemberment." Signed Jack

Max got up and stretched. He tried to walk toward Lucy, but he was stopped by something around his neck. (You and I would know it as a chain, but Lucy had never seen this device before. She had never seen anything that would restrict an animal's movements.

Since she had no idea what the dog would do next, she just kept very still and tried to hide herself better in the cattails.

The dog kept barking and barking

The dog kept pulling and pulling on the chain and barking, barking, barking.

Lucy was scared. She thought about flying away, but then she realized that she couldn't because of her sore wing.

That was a totally new thought. Flying away from danger was how she coped with the uncertainties of the world before. It's how every bird reacts to danger. But now, that was gone.

Lucy wiggled her way into the dense area of the cattails, hoping to hide from the dog. He stopped barking. Lucy had just learned a new lesson.

Her heart stopped racing.

The afternoon turned into evening and it got darker and darker. The big dog was now just a faint outline. Lucy could just make him out and it looked as if he was napping.

Lucy wondered how she would spend the night. It was now too dark to go wandering around in the pond. She realized she would have to spend the night in the water wedged in between the cattails.

She wiggled around a little bit to get herself better positioned for a night's sleep. Lucy was exhausted at this point and fell to sleep very quickly.

It was now too dark to go wandering around in the pond. She realized she would have to spend the night in the water wedged in-between the cattails.

But then she awoke to a slight noise. The snapping of a branch. She slowly turned her head to find the source of the noise.

A fox crept slowly toward her

But then she awoke to a slight noise. The snapping of a branch. She slowly turned her head to find the source of the noise. Off to her right she saw two tiny points of light. They were reflections from the street light off the eyes of a fox silently and slowly creeping toward her.

At this point, she dearly missed the protection of her flock. No matter if they were feeding or sleeping, one or two or more geese would always be on the lookout for danger. And if danger did approach they would call every bird's attention to it with a squawking and hissing sound. And angered geese can be a very potent force against any invading threat.

But now there was no protecting flock on the horizon and Lucy was alone. Very much alone.

The two spots of light from the fox's eyes grew larger and larger as he approached Lucy.

Lucy became frozen in fear. Finally she began thrashing and flapping her wings to try to gain flight and escape. But her damaged wing became tangled in the cattails and the more she struggled the more tangled she became. She involuntarily started

squawking and hissing as she
thrashed in the waters.

The fox was Max's enemy
The noise of the squawking and
thrashing awoke Max. And if he had
any enemy in the neighborhood, it
was the fox, who was always trying to
steal his food.

Max lunged toward those two white
spots of the fox's eyes. Barking and
growling. And churning up a foun-
tain of flying dirt as he dug away
at the ground with his front paws,
trying to free himself from his heavy
chain.

The two white reflections disappeared as the fox turned away. Even
though the fox knew that Max was
restricted because of the chain, he
made such a threatening noise, the
fox wasn't going to take any chances.
He slinked away into the darkness.

Lucy kept turning her head from
side to side, scanning the pond for
any new signs of danger. But all was
silent. Eventually, Max and Lucy fell
into a deep sleep.

The next morning was cloudy and
rainy. Lucy blinked several times as
she surveyed the pond, and remembered the very strange and somewhat
terrifying day before.

Off to her right she saw two tiny points of light. They were reflections from the street light off the eyes of a fox silently and slowly creeping toward her.

Geese always try to sleep in the center of a lake or large pond. They know that most of their predators, such as foxes and coyotes, can't swim very well.

A new life and surroundings
Her life had been completely turned
upside down.

On any other day, right now, she
would be comfortably in the center of
a flock of dozens and dozens of geese
as they nibbled away at the Skoda
cornfield. And then, as evening
approached, they would climb into
the sky to spend time in Bell's Pond, a
beautiful lake just a few miles away.

Geese always try to sleep in the
center of a lake or large pond. They
know that most of their predators,
such as foxes and coyotes, can't swim
very well. So they have safety during
the night on the pond.

The little pond didn't feel safe
The little pond she was in was just
too small to give her a feeling of
safety. A dog or wolf or coyote could
jump half-way across the pond and
catch her.

But right now, she was still in the
middle of a patch of cattails in this
tiny little pond at the bottom of the
hill. And it began raining harder and
harder.

She looked over at the dog house.
Max was stretched out taking a
morning nap. His owner came

over with a bucket full of meal and dumped it into Max's bowl.

Max looked up at his owner, stood up and shook off all the rain water that had been collecting on his back. He then went back into his dog house.

The rain began to come down in sheets. Lucy had experienced this before in the flock's trips far to the south during the fall season. The flock would be far, far up in the sky. Only visible as a series of V-shaped specs against the clouds.

The flock braved bursts of rain and lightning

But up in the clouds, the birds would be fighting terrible winds and bursts of rain and lightning. They had incredible courage and nothing seemed to deter them from their course. The birds would continue honking to encourage each other. And they would continue blinking to keep their eyes clear from the driving rain. Their attention was always centered on keeping their position in the flying V formation. And feeling the uplifting draft from the goose just in front.

The deluge of rain hitting her now brought back memories of these trips.

She looked at her left shoulder and

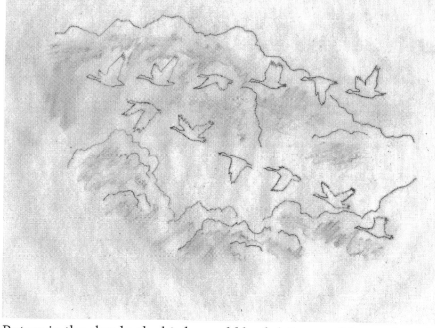

But up in the clouds, the birds would be fighting terrible winds and bursts of rain and lightning. They had incredible courage and nothing seemed to deter them from their course.

Max was watching. His head just outside his doorway to keep from getting drenched.

saw that it was now clear of the cat-tails. She pushed off with her webbed feet toward the center of the pond. Her wing was still sore, but her feet were in fine condition.

Lucy paddled toward the dog house. Her memories of these past flights and the rain now hitting her face gave her courage to explore the pond.

Was Max cheering her on?

Max was watching. His head just outside his doorway to keep from getting drenched. As Lucy crossed the pond from one side to another, Max would give out an occasional bark. But nothing mean-spirited. It was almost as if he was cheering her on.

After swimming for a long time, Lucy grew tired and looked for a place to rest. She looked toward the dog house. Max was silent and sat just staring at Lucy. She slowly pulled herself up out of the water just a few feet away from Max's house. She watched Max intently, but he didn't budge or even bark.

She sat down on the bank with a sigh, all the while looking in Max's direc-tion. It was still raining hard, and Max didn't want to leave his house and get all wet. Lucy never worried about getting wet. The rain drops just

rolled off her back, and her downy
feathers kept her dry underneath.

Max came roaring out of his house
All of a sudden, Max started barking
and came roaring out of his house,
churning up the ground as he went.

Lucy started honking and hissing and
ran down the hill into the water. She
was making a wake in the water as
she made her way back to the protection of her cattails.

Max was not running after Lucy,
thank goodness, but after a stranger
who had parked his car in the drive-
way and began walking toward the
owner's trailer.

But, he was stopped in his tracks by
Max's terrifying noises and his huge
black presence. Big, black and dan-
gerous looking, with a gigantic jaw
and glistening white teeth. And eyes
that shown like lasers.

Jack, the owner, came running out of
his trailer toward Max, yelling and
screaming. He grabbed Max's heavy
metal chain, hurled Max into his dog
house and slammed the door shut.

Jack then escorted his shaking visitor
to his trailer.

Lucy observed it all in silence from

All of a sudden, Max started barking and came roaring out of his house, churning up the ground as he went.

Lucy pecked on the door, again and again. First there was silence from the inside, but then Max whimpered.

her hideaway in the cattails. She stayed there for quite a while, afraid there might be another outburst.

Eventually, the visitor went back to his car and left Jack's property.

It wasn't until darkness approached that Lucy had the courage to leave her hiding and paddle over to Max's doghouse. She waddled up the bank and over to the door on his house.

Lucy pecked on the door, again and again

Lucy pecked on the door, again and again. First there was silence from the inside, but then Max whimpered. Lucy tapped again, and Max whimpered again.

She just sat there by the door through the night. All night long, there were soft cries from Max inside. Lucy stood guard over Max until the sun came up over the hill.

Lucy thought about all the lookouts in the flock who used to protect her. She was glad to be a lookout for Max.

The next day, Jack came over with food for Max. But he had something else in his hands. It was another bowl. Once he filled up Max's bowl, he put down the other plate. It had seeds in it. Jack then opened the door, and Max slowly came outside.

Max wolfed down his food, and then looked at the extra plate with seeds. It He wasn't interested. He just curled up and lay down near his door.

Lucy stared at the seed bowl for a few minutes. And then, her hunger took over. The seeds looked delicious. She nibbled a few. They were good. Then she started eating in all seriousness. Soon the plate was empty. She sat down on the grass near Max and joined him in a long sleep.

Max was licking his paw

When Lucy awoke, she noticed that Max was licking his front left paw. Licking, licking, licking. Something must have happened.

Max caught a splinter when Jack kicked him inside his dog house after Max terrorized Jack's visitor.

Lucy had amazing eyesight. Of course, all geese need to see just what's on the ground from thousands of feet up in the sky. Lucy clearly saw the splinter on the top of Max's left paw. She had an urge to pick at it. Geese do preen themselves most every day, straightening and cleaning their feathers. It's a primal urge.

But picking at the splinter would

Lucy stared at the seed bowl for a few minutes. And then,
her hunger took over.

Max licked his swollen paw a few more times and then lay down, resting his jaw on this paw.

mean getting closer to Max. He was still licking the spot where he picked up the splinter. After a few minutes, he looked away toward a noise he heard on the creek. Whenever Max's dog senses were alerted by a noise, 100 percent of his attention was focused on the direction of the noise. Nothing else existed.

In that moment, Lucy darted over to Max and plucked out the splinter with her beak. And just as quickly, she returned to her spot. Max didn't even know what had happened because Lucy moved so fast.

Max licked his swollen paw a few more times and then lay down, resting his jaw on this paw. He looked over toward Lucy and let out a long sigh. And then, he fell asleep.

Lucy and Max got to know each other better and better

The autumn days rolled on, and Lucy and Max got to know each other better and better. First of all, Lucy knew that Jack would feed her and Max every morning before Jack went to work.

Max would get a dish full of meat and kibbles and Lucy would get a dish full of wonderful grains and corn pellets.

Max also got a bowl of water because he couldn't reach the pond. He was on a chain. Of course, Jack knew that Lucy's movements weren't restricted. And that is why she didn't get a bowl of water because she could get all the water she wanted at the pond or the nearby creek.

Lucy had begun to explore her surroundings. There were afternoon swims in the creek. A small dam just down from Max's dog house created a large pool, in which she had swum back and forth many times. The water was cool and refreshing because it was always running. It came from the mountains far to the East.

In the mornings, Lucy preferred swimming in the pond because the still water there was warmer.

And Max was becoming a welcome friend. Lucy learned to ignore Max's terrifying outbursts when strangers approached. They were never aimed at her.

In fact, Max cherished Lucy's presence. Before she arrived, he had spent three years chained to his dog house with no one to share the day with. Nothing to look forward to except his bone, which he gnawed on constantly.

 A small dam just down from Max's dog house created a large pool, in which she had swum back and forth many times.

The only thing that Lucy missed was her flock and her bird friends.
They must be close to Virginia at this point in their fall flight

Now, Lucy and Max sat near each other for most of the day, sharing the sun and the rain.

Lucy missed her bird friends

The only thing that Lucy missed was her flock and her bird friends. They must be close to Virginia at this point in their fall flight. She remembered last year when the flock neared their winter grounds in Virginia. It was exciting to look down and know that is where they would be living for the next several months.

Lucy's wing was still sore, so that part of her life was no longer possible. She had accepted that, and her life now revolved around Max and the pond and the creek.

The warm days of fall soon turned cooler and ice began to form on the pond.

Day by day, the ice sheet spread across the pond. Each day, Lucy would waddle over the ice to the hole in the center. She could still dive to find nibbles at the bottom.

Lucy would just sit on the ice

And many times, Lucy would just sit on the ice. Her feet didn't get frost-bitten because of an ingenious system of arteries in her legs that nature had provided to most birds called Teria.

That, and the fact that there was little flesh in her legs and feet to freeze.

Max mostly just watched Lucy from his perch by his dog house. Nibbling on his bone. Only to be interrupted by a ferocious barking and a clawing of the earth if a stranger was passing by on the road.

Finally, the hole in the ice finally disappeared. Lucy came over to the center of the pond as usual, looking for her swimming hole. She paced back and forth, but it just wasn't there. Finally she turned and headed up the bank and sat down next to Max.

This required Lucy to make new sleeping arrangements. For her whole life, Lucy slept with the flock on a lake or pond. It was their protection because they knew that most of their predators could not swim. A portion of the flock was always awake to stand guard. And the guard assignments rotated amongst the geese. You slept for a while, and then you watched out for danger for a while.

And many times, Lucy would just sit on the ice.
Her feet didn't get frostbitten

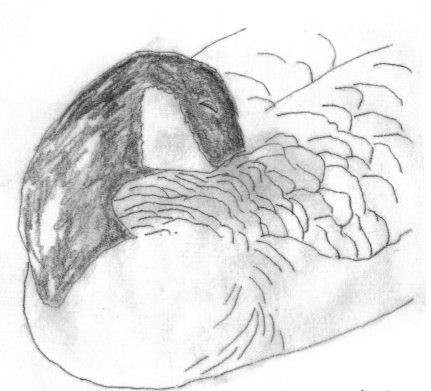

You could tell who was sleeping because a sleeping goose has its head turned with its bill tucked under its wing.

You could tell who was sleeping because a sleeping goose has its head turned with its bill tucked under its wing.

They made a perfect pair, sitting silently next to each other in the snow.

The snow got deeper every day
The snow got deeper every day, but Max kept digging away to create a clear spot where they could sit.

One winter's day Max and Lucy woke up to a blinding snow storm. They couldn't even see the pond from their perch near the dog house.

They waited for Jack to come with food and water dishes. He didn't come in the morning. He didn't come in the afternoon, nor that night.

And it continued to snow and snow and snow. By the second day, the snow was as high as the dog house. They felt like they were in an igloo.

By the afternoon of the second day they heard someone trudging through the snow. It was Jack. And he brought food. Max and Lucy were very hungry at this point.

For days and days, Max and Lucy lived in their igloo. Lucy had made a small path down the bank toward the pond. But there was no pond to be seen. You could not tell where the bank ended and the pond began.

Without food being brought to them every day by Jack, they would have starved. There was no food anywhere in sight.

The foxes and coyotes were hungry

But Lucy and Max were not the only ones who were hungry. The foxes and coyotes, too, were having difficulty finding small animals to eat. They were now all hidden under a huge blanket of snow.

One night, Max had not finished all of his food. It sat in his dish. And the smell of food must have been too much for a band of coyotes to resist. They had not eaten in days.

Max and Lucy could hear their cries.

They sounded like babies wailing. And they seem to have surrounded the pond and Max's dog house.

Lucy could not sleep. Instead, she instinctively stood guard, with her head erect, scanning the area from left to right.

Max started barking and growling. He knew the smell that coyotes gave off, and he knew that he needed to be on guard too.

But Lucy and Max were not the only ones who were hungry. The foxes and coyotes, too, were having difficulty finding small animals to eat.

Lucy began to flap her wings a little bit. Both of them. Her left wing was still a little sore, but at least she could move it now.

That is how they spent the night. All night long, the coyotes continued with their frightful cries. And all night long, Max and Lucy were on edge.

Finally, as morning approached, the howling stopped. And Max and Lucy fell into a deep sleep.

And that is how they made it through the winter. Lucy provided friendship for a very lonely dog. And Max provided security for an otherwise very vulnerable Lucy, who no longer had the protection of her flock.

Finally, the arrival of spring
The days grew longer and warmer, and finally, the ice melted on the pond. Lucy was once again able to forage for nibbles at the bottom of the pond.

During the summer months, Lucy began to flap her wings a little bit. Both of them. Her left wing was still a little sore, but at least she could move it now.

Every day, Lucy pushed off onto the little pond and flapped her wings as she began swimming with her webbed feet. Max watched intently from his perch by his house.

Her wing felt better and better every

day. And by midsummer she wasn't
feeling any pain at all. As she flapped her
wings, she began to lift herself
In the air. She kept paddling with her
feet to boost her body out of the water.

If you have never seen a flock of geese
taking off from a lake, you have missed
a funny site. It looks as if they're walking
on water as they paddle furiously to get
their bodies airborne.

Lucy had become airborne
One day as Lucy paddled and flapped
her wings, she was surprised to see that
she had became airborne. Yes, she was in
the air.

She wobbled a little bit but she was defi-
nitely airborne and headed up the hill
to her old feeding grounds on Skoda's
cornfield.

But her wings were feeling a little tired
so she thought she better head back to
Max's dog house.

As she approached, she saw that Max
was out of his doghouse and straining on
his chain and barking and wagging his
tail as he looked up at Lucy gliding down
to his pond.

Now every day brought a return visit to
that first flight up the hill to the cornfield. And back again to a very happy
Max, with his tail wagging in excitement.

If you have never seen a flock of geese taking off from a lake, you have missed a funny site. It looks as if they're walking on water as they paddle furiously to get their bodies airborne.

Lucy made repeated flights to the flock during the waning days of summer. Her wings grew stronger, and she began to feel more at home with the flock.

And every flight made her wings stronger and stronger. She no longer felt weak when she reached the top of the hill.

Lucy spotted her old friends

At the end of summer, she saw her old flock at Skoda's field. It was exciting to see them. Her old friend Judy was there, but Judy felt like a stranger.

Lucy landed on the field and began pecking at the fallen corn on the ground. She saw other birds that she recognized, but they also looked different.

Lucy flew back to the little pond down the hill. She saw Max waiting for her, wagging his tail.

Lucy made repeated flights to the flock during the waning days of summer. Her wings grew stronger, and she began to feel more at home with the flock. And as always, Max sat looking up the hill, waiting for Lucy's return.

One day Lucy joined the flock for its morning flight to Bell's Pond. It felt good to be on a big lake with all of her avian friends, and it felt good to have the protection of the flock.

She was now feeling a warmth and closeness to the flock.

The great fall flight to Virginia
Lucy heard talk that afternoon about the

great fall flight to Virginia. Everyone was excited by the prospect of the big move. Especially the new parents who were going to be bringing a clutch of baby geese with them.

A great sadness came over her

When she flew back to Max that afternoon a great sadness came over her. She could feel the pull that the flock had on her heart. It was something she couldn't express, but she could feel it.

Max was there as always, sitting up and straining his eyes to catch the first glimpse of Lucy as she glided down to their little pond. And wagging his tail.

The next morning Lucy took a leisurely paddle around their small pond, looking occasionally at Max as she went. Before she flew up the hill to be with the flock, she waddled up the bank to sit with Max, who was basking in the sun for his morning nap.

Then, she heard the honking of the geese as they took to the air from the top of the hill. She took one last look at Max before she walked into the pond, and then flew gracefully into the air.

But before she left the little pond area, Lucy circled around once and looked down. She could see Max sitting up and looking at her every movement.

Lucy met the flock at Bell's Pond, and they

But before she left the little pond area, Lucy circled around once and looked down. She could see Max sitting up and looking at her every movement.

climbed for over a thousand feet before they turned south to head for Virginia.

They crossed over Max and Lucy's little pond, and she could see a little dot on the ground. It was Max.

Lucy flew on for a few more miles, but she kept thinking of Max, sitting there waiting for her.

Too much for Lucy to bear
It was too much for Lucy to bear. Suddenly, there appeared a void in the flock's "V". And a lone Canadian Goose was seen leaving the flock and gliding in a long graceful arc back to a little pond by the side of a creek at the bottom of a hill in Taghkanic, New York.

THE END

Author © Dan Udell

★★★★★

'Geese don't walk down roads,'
March 28, 2016, By Grady Harp

This review is from: Lucy & Max: A mostly true story about the amazing friendship between a wild goose and a 'ferocious' guard dog in Taghkanic, New York (Kindle Edition)

"New York State author Dan Udell has that kind of life that embraces all things of the mind and soul – music, writing, photography, science, technology and the wonders of nature. He earned degrees in physics and mathematics form Rensselaer Polytechnic Institute, offered his talent as a writer with IBM (science, technology and photoessays and videography presentations for historic events), and curated art exhibitions as well as being the featured artist in many solo photographic exhibitions. Now, turning to a novel/memoir medium he places before us one of the more unusual and fascinating true stories – LUCY AND MAX –a very unusual pairing of the canine and avian worlds, an inexplicable goose and dog alliance, true and lasting.

"In this completely charming rather short tale Dan Udell combines black and white drawings of both of his main characters, Lucy the goose and Max the dog, with beautifully spaced floating paragraphs telling us of the 'accidental' meeting of Lucy (who suffered a broken wing during fall flight) and Max chained to his dog house, their gradual building of trust and respect and protection from 'outsider' animals as well as Jack (Max's owner), and through the narration by Dan we learn of the idiosyncrasies of this strange but very tender and understated relationship between goose and dog. We travel the seasons together, learn of encounters with outsiders and the growing relationship that forms so that when Lucy's wing finally heals and she can once again fly, the ongoing relationship continues.

"It is as quiet and lovely as that, but the beauty of the story is the unexpected innocence and friendship that proves that colleagues and friends are where you find them – despite what the outside world may think! A beautiful little melody of nature told and illustrated with elegance and love.

Highly Recommended. Grady Harp, March 16."

photo credit: Mary Udell at Bash Bish Falls, MA

Dan Udell is a modern-day Renaissance Man, spanning the worlds of science and technology as well as writing, music, photography and videography. A lover of nature from early childhood, Udell grew up in the now populated suburb of Westchester, NY, when ancient farms covered the landscape. Long hikes and bike trips introduced him to the wonders of the natural world.

His career included studies of the sciences, where he graduated from Rensselaer Polytechnic Institute in Troy, NY with degrees in physics and mathematics. He combined those interests with a passion for writing at IBM, where he was a science and
technology writer for many years. He was IBM's chief spokesperson for all its products; worked with famed photographer, Henri Cartier Bresson on a photo essay, "Man and Machine;" worked with John Sculley, past Apple CEO on a major IBM/Apple/Motorola alliance; explained the inner workings, to the press, of IBM computers on Space Shuttle during its first four launches at Cape Canaveral, and created many worldwide announcements, photo and video landmarks, now residing at MIT's Museum and San Franciso's Exploratorium, among others.

He teamed up with his wife, Mary Udell to help curate art exhibits for her exciting, and peripatetic, Sound Shore gallery in the New York and Connecticut area, and was also represented in many one-person and group shows of photography. His photographs are represented in the collections of PepsiCo, GE, Merrill Lynch, then-MCI, Benerofe Properties and other corporations and private holdings.

His new book, "Lucy and Max," looks at a very unusual pairing of the canine and avian worlds, a relationship he observed during his walks with Dan and Mary's dog, "Inky." It was an inexplicable goose and dog alliance, but still true and lasting.

Made in the USA
Middletown, DE
21 April 2016